MOON ON ROAM

MOON ON ROAM

Poems

MELISSA BARRETT
Gold Wake Press

Copyright © 2019 by Melissa Barrett

Published by Gold Wake Press

No part of this book may be reproduced
except in brief quotations and in reviews
without permission from the publisher.

10 9 8 7 6 5 4 3 2 1

Moon on Roam
2019, Melissa Barrett

goldwake.com

TABLE OF CONTENTS

NOON SAYS NO TWICE	3
MY LIFE	4
THE BRAIN NAMES ITSELF	5
LIVED ON DECAF, FACED NO DEVIL	6
CROSS-EXAMINATION	8
MOTHER IS ONLY ONE LETTER FROM	9
WINE DARK & SEE THRU	10
PARACLETE	11
GRAVITY & GRAVES	15
DEATH DIE DEAD	16
WFM: ALLERGIC TO PINE-SOL, AM I THE ONLY ONE	17
PRY THE LID OFF THE TERRARIUM	18
ASBESTOS AT BEST	19
YES IS NOT THE ONLY LIVING THING	20
THE FRENCH INTERIOR AS THE VOICE OF TRAUMA	21
SKINNY WISDOM	22
RHYMES WITH THIGH GAP	23
OPRAH'S DOWRY	24
"MAYBE, MAYBE" (MEANING MAYBE NOT)	25
MIRACLE BABY BORN WITH A JOB	26
V.D.	27
WARLIER	29

•

IF I WERE THE MOON, I KNOW WHERE I WOULD FALL DOWN	33
BOY EATING ICE	34
HER SOUL HAD NO STRIPES	36
WINCHESTER TRILOGY	37
FORGETTING I'D ALREADY FORGOTTEN	42
POOR SELF OF STEAM	43
PONDS OF BLONDES	44

A FRENCH INTERIOR	45
MORE MATTER WITH LESS ART	46
WHY OUR APARTMENT SHOULD BECOME MY APARTMENT AGAIN	47
THE VOICE OF TRAUMA	49
MORE PRAISE FOR STEPHEN KING	50
RED BADGE OF COURAGE	51
I AM BOTH WORSE AND BETTER THAN YOU THOUGHT	53 53
DEFINITIONS OF EXCESS	54
MISS NEEDLES & THE DIVORCE	55
YOURS	56

for Pete

NOON SAYS NO TWICE

Whirled says he and led and in real life.
Piece says nothing wholly, only fractions
of ice. Mary says holy lowly wholesome me.
Pearl says ear and pear but never pier.
Everything by definition encompasses everything
except it has just two e's. E.E. I'm coming.
There must be more in the trees:
evergreen cedar eastern et cetera. We've already
disgust how language is dumbing. Thunder
thunders. A boy so awkward even his jeans
stutter. I'm weary of it. I'd wear that. War
changes maps. Even MLK played Mortal Kombat.
Finish him to the tune of a Finnish hymn,
Raaka Kypsennetty. Give me oral—
how people used to ask for story. Back when horny
described a Viking's hat. Leifs and rubbers
congeal in the gutter: rub them together and start
a fire. Sartre says art and almost retard.
Stars aren't close, but clothes are yarn.
Brains vs. brawn vs. bronze-flecked fawns.
Vs. says us, and guess who won.

MY LIFE

Instead of buttering the lobster, I'm abutting the bolster
Instead of a charcoal slab, I'm slow in the bath
Instead of brushing and braiding, I'm a shrub near a drain
Instead of knots in the netting, I'm ten tons of nothing
Instead of cutting some calories, I'm a contrail in Calcutta
Instead of getting a bus pass, I'm Gus with a box cutter
Instead of poor etiquette, I'm petting a quiet pet
Instead of rereading Nightwood, I would dread every night
Instead of cracking a mirror, I hear a mere cackle
Instead of a worse horse, I'm rehearsing the war
Instead of getting rug burn, I'll be on a gurney
Instead of a low pool, I'm a loophole you'll pull
Instead of a daffodil, I'm a lid full of dill, folded and dull
Instead of being lonely, I'm only a little

THE BRAIN NAMES ITSELF

The brain named Leif Erikson and Verizon.
Named our dog After after *after,* my favorite
preposition. The brain named looners, nooners,
and euphemisms. Brought an al dente noodle
to the spaghetti house. The brain invented paint by numbers
with Bob Ross and painted numbers on wooden cubes
and a wood of painted bark. It invented acronyms
and contractions. DTF at two o'clock. The brain
invented measurements for precise timekeeping
and the idea that time is a social construct.
The brain thinks a thought and thinks about thinking.
You don't get much more meta than a fruit salad
served from a watermelon basket. The brain wrote
the heaventree of stars hung with humid nightblue fruit.
The brain traced lines from stars and starred the best lines
from books. The brain wrote books and turned some
into props, like the hollowed-out Bible that held alcohol
in The Simpsons. The other Homer spoke his books
and hollowed out a horse. The brain named Zima, Zafiro
Añejo, Helen, and the hippocampus, which comes
in the shape of a seahorse. The brain invented comparison.
The brain invented cramming. The brain invented irony.
Imagine all the med students trying to commit
the functions of the hippocampus to memory.

LIVED ON DECAF, FACED NO DEVIL

Around the same time that umbrellas went comfortably co-ed,
you could walk the wet bridge without query, without
being called queer, without the rain finding that quiet cadent
part of you. Right around the time The Umbrellas was painted:
all those plump, chalked-up cheeks. Pre-, post-, and all throughout
bad art but before the telescopic folding umbrella ensconced
our best gentlemen like silky attics—what a strange invention,
from the French, *ombrelle*. Of course it'd catch. Except with
the Puritans, who spurned it because the rain is rain is rain is
Jesus Christ. Which was right around the time the Baron Jejeebhoy
was busy distributing his lots to the poor. In 1858, that should
have been the fashion. In 1958, it should have been law.
One hundred and two years before I was told that history repeats
itself, but only the bad history, causing every window in my life
to shatter, again. So the rain fell harder: the gutters churning,
worms upending—hours later the puddles were clouds
because everything gets flipped around like that. Like my little
cousin Hannah, the brat: named the same way forward and back.
Ninety-two thousand years before the dogbrella should have never
been invented. Thirty-two minutes ago I walked my dogs in the rain,
Puritan-like. When time travel is real, I'll walk them to the hall tree
where Bliss's jacket hangs drizzly with spinal fluid. Make him
suck on a Carbolic Smoke Ball. Or the Gdańsk Time Ball,
which was considered technology once. And then the big war
started: the *second* one. I told you: only the bad history.
And we never listen to living history, says Gramps
who fought in all the wars and walked uphill both ways.
So he winds his watch but reads the porcelain dial backwards.
Miasma is a good example: it was science before it wasn't, and now
you need a permit to spray Glade in LA. Three hours before
Mount Lister will become a frail raft, deleveled, speck of a speck,
I'll drain my Listerine in the bay. Most people obsess over time,
but not like this. I was raised in a house with more than

4,000 pocket watches and clocks: a pendulum swings
in my chest. They're building amphibious homes now—
houses suitable for frogs. The carbon is my heart
burning like a goldenrod-adorned log.

CROSS-EXAMINATION

Memory at its finest is the lipreading of a lost moment.
Instead of "I love you," you got "island view." Instead
of "my tag is itchy," you make out "my dad's an intern."
Well, my dad *is* an intern, so that's lucky. Read my lips:
I'm a good liar. I think this is because I have a round face.
Cherub cheeks and eyes that disappear when I laugh:
something about all that tells people I am "innocent."
You get away with a lot if you have the right bone structure.
Studies show that people who use air quotes are full of shit.
Other studies show that people who curse openly
tend to be more honest, that women who wear makeup
are perceived as being more trustworthy. Figure that one out.
Here is a fact proven by science: 100 percent of writers
are "storytellers." As in, dishonest people. It's like what
Amy Hempel said: similes are liars, and metaphors
are better liars. Nothing in the world is truly like anything else
so why do we insist on drawing comparisons? Except she
didn't say it exactly like that. I don't remember what she said
or if I was even in the room to hear her say it. Eyewitness testimony
is about as reliable as my mailman, who told me there's something
kind of sexy about always being late. Perjury is defined as knowingly
making a false statement. Merely misremembering is not a crime.
How many of us misremember the first line of this poem?
In the dark auditorium, after the applause, the poet sits down
as the audience scrambles to recall a favorite line. The memory
of her lips reading lost. You lean over and tell me,
"You just touched my thigh." Watching your mouth move,
I get, "You look deep in thought." I swear to God,
I am deep in something. I just don't know what.

MOTHER IS ONLY ONE LETTER FROM

Homer, the father of culture. And yet he was never born.
And yet he gave birth to a hero who wanted to go home.
Home. Two letters. Let her journey, too. Culture. One letter from
ulcer. A moth laying eggs on your good suit. On the suitor's leather.
The books on motherhood change every year, but they all say
there will be blood. Saddam Hussein popularized the expression
  "the mother of all ——— "
when he referred to the Gulf War. The first one. The second
was his redheaded stepson. All wars create gulfs, and all wars
are motherly, since from death comes life. Cf. forest fires.
They're part of a forest's natural ecology. From death comes heat.
From heat comes tea. Find our way back to this scene, carrying
  a knife, a camera, a book of myths.
That's Adrienne Rich. My children cause me the most exquisite
suffering. Poor Penelope. It's not easy being the first cocktease,
the original single mom. She suffered, too. Molly Bloom
said yes I said yes I will Yes. What hyperbole. And Penelope,
No. Please. Smothered by the suitors, the rumors, fidelity,
a son. T is for Telemachus, two letters from machetes.

WINE DARK & SEE THRU

Is a crimson jersey, all the little holes.
Is a criminal jury, all the empty hope.
Is a hoe, and horror, and whore or
house. Is a crimp in the journey, a permed
boy scout. Beat him red or beat him
off—unlace his cleats, jockstrap off.
The Jockyssey was a straight-to-DVD feature.
Shark blue and sea thru is more accurately
water. Is how I like my coffee, my men,
all their little holes: poured full of sweat
and bored of brunettes. Our mascot is a jersey cow
pouring a glass of milk. I like Kool-Aid, too.
Wine dark and see thru. Is a wrestler's throat,
slashed by a razor stuffed under the mat.
The Matt. The moat. The Trojans always murder us.
Maraud us major time. What a deep throat you have
jock. What a tiny Boston crab. Little red
ride me good, pointy and jumping like a laser.

PARACLETE

Once, I was so patient.
Once, I was mousy and tender and I put out always.
Once, you ought to have seen me growing up in that teeny house
    with the five babies and Mom just died and Dad thought
    Jesus came back to Earth in the year 70 AD.
Once, I had the cracking and busted-up hands of a poor farmer.
Once, I was a mother at the age of nine.

This is the period I will refer to as my "actual insanity."
My "internment." My "lonelymaking."
Also known as my horrible secret, continent-wide.

You know that expression—all good things
must be annihilated. Well, lesions split up behind my ears
like slugs inking their way toward my eyes.
I soon became blind. Blind and simultaneously

able to understand everything perfectly. I was the most
intelligent person in Illinois, and so it was with ease
that I discovered that I lived in a prison inside of a prison.

With the dawn of my intelligence, my husband (he's a lawyer,
he examines land) called on an alienist. The alienist
asked me to empty my pockets. I dramatically turned
my pockets completely inside out.

What could I have? What have I *ever* had?

I had a little teeny tiny silver-plated bell in my breast pocket.

During my internment, I was as silent as:

        the crown molding, which was unpeeling.

> as: the land my husband examines—
> all that red peanutly dirt.
> as: kneading. And *needing*.

The alienist held out his hand expectantly.

I clutched the little bell until I felt its clapper slide against
        my palm—this I intuited as a request.
I clutched the little bell until it pulverized.

And the alienist—he—he—forcibly unclenched my fist, dumped the powder into his drawstring pouch, and then—he—licked between my fingers all the rest of that fine babyblue dust.

He insisted on looking me dead in the eyes while he was licking.

(He did not know that I identified as *blind*.)

But! I had another bell. An invisible bell that *I saw in my mind*—
and I could listen to it just by blinking.

When I slept, a clatter of angel hair wound itself around me.
When I slept, no one in the world would lick my fingers.

Pretend for a minute that you are me.

Pretend the papers have declared your husband to be a horse's ass.
Pretend your brother wrote *The Bible: Part II*.
Pretend your brother once chased you with an axe, and then murdered the president.

And by "the president" I mean *The President*.

For how many seconds could you remain contrite and
        hummingbirdlike?

And then please recall how I flitted around like a hummingbird for *decades*. For roughly all my life.

This is why I was able to give my body up to that asylum. My body but not my mind. You know the old saying—

Mind over your pasty waterlogged limbs.

Yes, they tried to drown it out of me.
Some new experimental "treatment"—

My feet were permanently pruned,
my ankles forever blue,
my body altogether hairless and stooping.

They say the lack of empathy is a dead-ringer for insanity.

I have a new theory:

Too much empathy will singe a small hole, just barely noticeable,
into your soul and each day you live your magnanimous life,
the hole grows and it grows until eventually it becomes a universe

and every piece of you sinks toward its bottom,
which is a giant rusted drain inexorably swallowing all of you.
Your consciousness is last but it, too, slips through

and the only thing left is the one tear you saved, your final lament

for the state of the world, and when that dribbles out—truly, truly you are left with nothing.

It will also ruin a marriage.

My most empathetic gesture was the day I walked those dirt floors
       to your holding cell,
my bouquet smiling up into your tired pink eyes:

nasturtium, gladiola, sunflowers, the dandelion heads

snapped off and floated up, a symbol of hope, some promise
      of brightness—

I've never been as tender as the day I asked you to end your life.

GRAVITY & GRAVES

>—*No man is an island,* John Donne
>—*No woman is an islandess,* Alice Notley

No woman is an *I'll*
and no man is ground
-ed emotionally. Nearly dead
inside, men, though babies
(girls and boys) cry at
the same rate. Men with
no interior and women
with no criteria more grave
than mothering: *I'll be*—
I'll do—I'll have eight
cradles ready and waiting
for a vapid dad and his saplings.
So many siblings! Gravid
and new, my uterus blooming
so vastly it's hard to have
grace. Gravity of the womb
then the growing-up blues.
Young skulls sulk and
unspool: childhood's ending.
A sullen generation slowly
growing, groveling, owing . . .
must be time for another wedding.

DEATH DIE DEAD

To all the protectors of children out there: Why bother.
Here's a note I found on the floor of a sixth-grade classroom:
ARE YOU A VERSION. They can't even spell.
You know that Lord of the Flies book. Those kids
killed Simon. He was the best character. So what
if I would have done the same thing. So what if I used to yell
I WISH YOU WERE DEAD to everyone I loved.
When I was little, I'd play a game with my sisters and brother
called Death Die Dead. Wielding plastic axes, we'd skate around
the basement and fake murder each other. We were too safe
in our cuteness, we knew nothing about life. Another example
is Macon Dead. He was a real brat. He didn't want to become
a doctor because he didn't want the initials MD, MD.
The kid in me thinks there's not a better reason than that.

WFM: ALLERGIC TO PINE-SOL, AM I THE ONLY ONE

—lines from personal ads

Hi. I react really badly to Pine-Sol. My eyelids swell up and my eyes
turn bright red. I am a REAL woman. It is January 1st.
Educated men move to the top of the list. We were both
getting gas Wednesday evening. Fish counter, Giant Eagle:
My husband knows how attractive I find you.
You caught me singing loudly. Your name means "wind."
This Christmas season marks my eighth year of being single.
Please have a car (truck preferably) and a job.
I collect candles and have two grown children who are
on their own now thank God. I already bought your birthday present—
it's a tie. With swordfish on it. There are certain things
my nose can't handle and smoking is one of them.
I signed up to volunteer at a local park for a Merry-not-Scary
trick-or-treat trail—it would be nice to have a companion.
Must be willing to be seen in public with a size 16 woman.
Six one four five nine eight two three one nine. I can swing
a hammer and am a pro at putting on make-up. Sexiness
to me is you plus a photographic memory. Do you have questions
you've always wanted to ask a woman? You left your receipt
and that's how I figured out your name. I was behind you
at the Lane Avenue Starbucks drive thru and you paid
for my grande nonfat no whip Mocha Frapp.
Your silver hair was gorgeous. Wow. The first time
we made love our souls connected and intertwined
and seemed to remember they were destined for one another.
Let's go to the shooting range. I have no business expertise,
but I'd love a guy who is good with rope.

PRY THE LID OFF THE TERRARIUM

Tear that cactus out of the sand. It's time to plant
some tulips, which is slang for giving head. You know,
like plant your purple two lips on my bearded clam.
Pry the lid off the terrarium. Give the clams back
to the sea. My new life goal is to live unshelled, calmly
only me. Pry the lid off your left atrium. Let your heart
thump finally free. Ideally you won't die but there is
no guarantee. Try to listen more to nature, to wager
more on stars. Start a club for gazing at Orion, or
at Kevin Bacon in Apollo 13. Pry the hood off
my Chevy Terraplane, cherry red with the original glass.
Drive the kids to banned camp, where they'll score
The Grapes of Wrath. Social class is static, but no one
knows the math. Pry the lid off my worldview.
I want to hate division, but I don't have
the poverty to. Let the middle class eat diamonds.
Pry the taxes off my portfolio by disbursing it in the sea
surrounding the Cayman Islands. It's critical that
the 1 percent reach a critical mass. Total divination
is diabetic greenbacks devoid of giving back.

ASBESTOS AT BEST

That February when the cat was timorously tumorous and the sky
was Tylenol-white. Go write it in your

travelogue, the voice on TV says. I'm watching The Truman Show.
My definition of excess?

Christof's weather manipulator stationed on the moon. Also,
dog treats in the shape of tiny toothbrushes.

Millennials are the worst. They're on a mission to make the hyphen
obsolete. They care a lot about trigger warnings

and Target. How many mechanics does it take to fix a busted-up
Taurus? Zero. All Tauruses are broken

beyond repair; it's the worst astrological sign. Millennials
are self-centered, but they don't put

the hyphen in. Hitler was a Taurus. He drove a Volkswagen.
If I were floored, I'd want to be

carpeted. If I were the ground, I'd want to be a crater
on Christof's moon, Tylenol-white.

If I were Canada, I'd mine and export asbestos for 130 years, too.
If I were a cat, I'd breathe it all in.

YES IS NOT THE ONLY LIVING THING

So be it. So bring it, South Beach Diet. So behave or better
don't. So long sobriety—it's social drinking week and I'm
historically thirsty. Sloe gin till my vision twins while solid
mental grace singes a hole (that's classic YES and modern no):
Slowly, solicitously, Juano unbuttons a butterfingered solo.
The university's golden podium assembled to dismember
Phi Psi machismo: mic's broke and the Take Back the Night
speaker's only so-so. So, so still: Consent: that yes: truly
pivotal. Get it, or wait patiently pinching mistletoe.

THE FRENCH INTERIOR AS THE VOICE OF TRAUMA

I would have tackled the guys. Sacked 'em. I would have
knocked 'em flat out. Says everyone who had no role at all
in 9/11. If I were on that plane, if I were accused, accosted,
if I were in any type of challenging situation at all, if I were
Alex Trebek, I would have never have shaved. I'll take
Movember for $600, Alex. What the fuck is it.
What is all this solidarity behind facial hair. What is solid
but also a liquid? A pitcher of sweet tea, but not a picture
of sweet tea, which is actually nothing, like all pictures,
sweetie. Talk about excessive. Talk about drowning.
I never believed you could drown in a teaspoon of water
till I saw the world's largest spoon. Till I drowned a gnat.
I didn't mean to. I want to be the big spoon, I tell
my boyfriend, but I'm lying. I don't have a boyfriend.
I have a *partner*. He makes art. Pictures. He slept through 9/11.
He has a beard like a swath of black and white ants.
On bad days, he says things like, "I make things and they are just things
and I'm sick of making things." What if the gnat had babies
to take care of. What if the planes missed. What if his face
really were scrawled with ants. What if all art is useless.

SKINNY WISDOM

When someone says, "Do your worst" to me,
I give them a Montessori education
and a gluten-free pancake.

Color psychology is my life. Watches are gold
because time is the real currency.
Barns are red because farmers want us to stop

tagging pictures of farm-to-table brunches.
I appear to crave independence but really
I just want to read your blog. Braid my hair

and feed me cold tofu. When Dostoevsky wrote
that beauty will save the world, I don't think
he meant to inspire a Dove commercial.

When I watched that Dove commercial,
I didn't mean to get turned on.
A recent study found that straight women

are most attracted to men with strong
immune systems and resistance to hepatitis B.
I'm most attracted to those with no resistance

to general misshapenness. To catfish accounts.
Beowulf was the original Bae. The first baby
named Brexit was born in South Beach today.

RHYMES WITH THIGH GAP

Why don't we call it a whore*home*. Or
a rustic slut cottage. A sleazy French
chateau. How easy is it to dress up
undressing. To elevate the taboo.
Add an adverb like harmoniously,
subtract the verb screw. Who hasn't
artfully photographed their nude body?
Positioned an Ikea lamp to illuminate
a thigh gap? I'd love a relief map
of so many bodies. Ovaries are the size
of almonds and a uterus grows to become
a hotel lobby. Meanwhile a boner looks
like Thailand, kind of. I love Thai food.
Thighs with or without the gap. Flat
brimmed snapbacks. Freud tells us
everything is a sexual object, even
thimbles and speed traps. Even neglect
and the Myers-Briggs test. Swiss citizens
supposedly have the world's best sex, and
with very low rates of disease. Not surprising.
Who doesn't like to slide their tongue
through the holes in Swiss cheese?

OPRAH'S DOWRY

Red thread and an old gold glove and
A strand of dread treading here: unwed
Stedman said, I skidded off that ledge
Incredulous, like most banned books I was
Misread. Mistaken for a weed that never
Stopped spreading. For being clever, it was
Over. Wish I could have been clover, lived
Closer, chosen for love and not cloistered
Like a lover. A loser. I lost everything.
Loosen the rumors. My poor bulldozed
Future. Unstitch these fat sutures. Unhitched
And severed from success (but not sex) said
No man about not having a wedding ever.

"MAYBE, MAYBE" (MEANING MAYBE NOT)

Senseless is monogamy, fat innocence
is love. Since I'm married, my husband
finishes my sentences. Don't be so
serious we say at the exact same time. He wishes
to be a senator, which means he's dull and white.
I have four kids, so I thought it sensible
to marry. I was right. Mary the mother of God
stood sentry on our wedding night. I'm not too
sentimental, but marriage set me right.
Every young lady needs a sentencer—
someone to center her. Mentor and enter her.
A stand-up, make-the-world-better kinda guy.
Mr. Right is essentially reticent. Sensuality is nice
but not required. Someone who makes more
than seventy-seven cents to a dollar, who concedes nothing
and can shoot a revolver. A good husband
is biologically evolved. He's taller. His face is stern
and stye-less; his muscular system revered.
Central to him is his career at Century 21.
True he's not very sensitive—he censures, censors,
resents, wants revenge, and shuns others—and he's
often too austere. He's overrepresented and complacent
with it all, dissenting only ever in an absentminded
kind of way. But maybe, maybe I'll settle.
After all, he walks the Irish Setter twice a day.

MIRACLE BABY BORN WITH A JOB

in a pecan orchard, Georgia, cigarette breaks
included. I regret I had to ask

is it ageist to say _____?
My voice pert and lucid, having learned to speak

in a town where the worst crime was my own
baldness. A little more bacon grease

for the fritter, toss some butter in that taco salad.
What else is buried there, under

the mulch? My neighbor's husband, beard
tough as lace. Brute hands grip-trained, arm hair

sprung into brilliant black wreaths. We're getting
our fences put in on the same day: next month,

a Tuesday. We're sanding columns with our own
raunchy laughter and the pollution is killing me.

V.D.

Fluorescent lighting so loud we lose
Our hearing, so loud

It says its name: Bright, bright—
An auditorium

Of tear-stained yesses and my skin
The color of vichyssoise,

A mattress left out in the rain.
The pleather is wet

With venereal disease tonight
And tomorrow

Every newspaper will slowly
Go broke. Give us

Half mast for the obit, o please.
This is the year

Broadsheet could keep us from
The icecaps, almost

A cure for homesickness if only
We hadn't forgotten

How to read. Ms. Loren, let your
Poor face

Retire—that legacy of tenth grade
Bulimia and winged

Eyeliner won't die, it races through
Us like Theraflu, like

Commitment even though marriage
Ruins our email

Contacts. Like the horses in Westerns
We stand: deferring

To a ring of too-serious actors—
Meanwhile

Everything in Black Hawk dies
Or grows

Tokens. Home is a green dusk,
A rim of woods

And our wooden owl at the cornice,
Never knowing flight.

WARLIER

A typo, I meant earlier, but apt for a country
that coins terms to match
the goals of its military, a *highly weaponized*
anything, a place of discounted day-old
baked goods, a stream of As in June
exchanged for movie rentals
or bowling shoes and a basket of jumbo maxi
pads on the counter in the bathroom, just help
yourself. These are the things we aim to protect.
A country with a language like a stop
watch going in a drawer, and my own words
corroborated by that signal. The sky a twist
of rope, fat and wet, weighing down Bowman
Field, past shadows of single-passenger planes
that sting the ground in a fuzz of violet.
My old professor, a ring of silver hair circling
his head, told me he wasn't ready to show
his grandchildren monuments that glorified war.
We walked through the National Mall
past trashcans sculpted high with plastic.
A country that organizes its trash
but it's still trash. And in the very best case
it will become trash once again. It's like
how Merwin ended his poem "When the War
is Over"—he said, "We will all enlist again."

IF I WERE THE MOON, I KNOW WHERE I WOULD FALL DOWN

In the caked oak tracts of the thumbed dim
chalkboard, behind the easel tipping paler
continents further north, toward the gloss
    of April, let it be April,
toward the unsmearing concrete breaks
for the searing purslane, to the basement
    to my father—forestly, forgetful
whistling to an unhitched Carolina dark,
to a treeline wading, I said trees are waiting
and swing sets corroding everywhere
in this state (our license plate art
    is acid rain), let me go
into the church—alone: so much volition
in that tower's toothed space. I'll fall there,
hit the chin of the moon's stannic oatmeal
face, but aim for the garden, splaying out
    in splayed spades.

BOY EATING ICE

It is his gift,
   at this age when his torso
is longest, twenty years old and cinching
     right up to a ridge
of skin, every bit of him
        pitched
around a coil of crucial organs—
that locketed holy mesh
home of *pit* and *pat*.

Once I bought dinner
for a boy who drank a large Sprite
   just to get to
the ice: his jaw
never stopped. When I see this boy's
confident bank of teeth
    going, boulders

    touch boulders. It's
convincing someone who never
once believed.

   In fealty, he gives
up so much, just looking—
       a faunlet, with winter apple eyes . . .
I told myself I loved him.
      I was right.

      I think
of the governance of woman
  when I see the boy before me, his ribs
stacking like plinths—
         of women

who learn to live in a circumference

of dime, and boys
              in whole fields of loosestrife.

 The wind lifts
    each piece of his hair
as it lifts each soft
        sorghum head, a vault
 of sky widens:

    You've always wanted
        to be that effortless

But I'm slight, scurrying
  against granite, against
this stillborn November—

 My chest a well
of cold air: *Go Go Go*
       it says . . .

Even when I guide my own hand
I feel like I'm pinning something down.

HER SOUL HAD NO STRIPES

I asked you what you wanted from all this and your jump rope
Stopped, skidded to gravel,
Your voice suddenly cold, antiseptic, marching out in blue ovals,
The braid between us
Undone, shook out in a smash of grass, an American lawn
Lumped and bunched
From cutworm tunnels, my eyes on the puddles, proud
With the bait of a sharp little moon.
It was so quiet, so urgent, the one thing I'd stitched to my tongue.
But the words were bricked
In, à la Plaza Mayor in Madrid. Like a drowning, a vagueness
Poured out over every
Poorly lit crib. Sad little things, you obsessed mid-yawn, mid-sin.
Such a big garage you've got
And no room to forgive. Well . . . it's complex. My definition
Of excess? Spelling *s*
E-s-s. This is what I want, you said, folding the rug we sat on
Into a pleated peplum dress.

WINCHESTER TRILOGY

Tell me again. About the ocean,
how the sun
never returned to Venice Beach.

> *Our cottage pink with candlelight.*
> *So soft the shadows*
>
> *almost evaporate.*
>
> *Eventually the moon gets so tired,*
> *it just pulls the tide*
> *right up to our door.*

The sand's ignored
BEWARE OF THE UNDERTOW signs.

> *And the musk of a swelling tide.*
>
> *The fronds paddle toward us*
> *and then get slammed into the mat*
> *of a rock-ribbed shore.*
>
> *Beach glass dripping*
> *in violet coronation.*

Stars fall like sprinkles. They're
five-pointed, cut from paper.

Everything is two-dimensional.

> *Except fear.*

What is fear?

*Dearheart, you know better than
me. Winchester was made of it.*

*Children love it. Or rather, they
love rescue. We develop insecurities*

*to be reassured by our securities.
To be mollified. Loved.*

*The most unloved people are also
the most scared.*

Are you scared?

*I'm scared of all the normal things.
Bush. California zombies and
California capitalists.*

*The hierarchal pseudo-religious
henchmen. Shitty art.*

Tell me the nightmare.
The one you have when
you're awake.

*It's fever-inducing. Terrestrial.
With flashes, flashes every second.*

Because they've built these mirrors.

Mirrors three stories high.

*And the flashes collide with each
other—so you see yourself
at every angle, pieced together,
neon, in a network*

         of endless permutations—you,

         appraised by an ohmmeter.
         It's total cultural vertigo.

Why are they doing it?

         Because we are beautiful, they
         think we are vain.

         They hate art.

         They hate original thought.

I'll get a gun.

         Their surveillance network
         is vast and impenetrable.

Even here, in the rectory?

         Living in a church . . .
         it's almost safe.

         That's why I plant with the
         pastor. Why I organized
         the fundraiser. Why I help
         with the laundry.

The wine stain,
like a rodent's skull.

         Anything can be anything else.
         This flashlight, for example,
         can easily become a club, a baton.

         Medicine, poison.

*Crackling static now
your urgent message.*

And the flashes can be fireworks.

Fireworks like garland
sagging onto the balcony.

It's not so easy.

*It's true that language created even
the first ever illumination,*

*and now we borrow back a little
word and a little wattage—*

but evil does not just become good.

*And the realization that your
ripest fear is manufactured*

does not set you free.

What about death and life.

The only way to bridge those two

is to end it yourself.

The only way?

*Surveillance is irreversible. More
irreversible than death.*

I know. I know.

The emerald waves,
when they seal above my head,

are your arms.

*I hoped, but didn't know, you'd
follow me.*

That morning I prayed for rain.

*To become a shape. A clot.
To return to the bleary elemental.*

*I just couldn't be a person
anymore.*

FORGETTING I'D ALREADY FORGOTTEN

Now it's back, dragged back, up the steps, crawled
over, stood up, ready to be seen—here, by accident.
REMEMBER ME etched into a gold-plated locket.
Happy anniversary, little dear. Only one more month
before the annulment. Smell triggers more memories
than any other sense, even sight. I'm attempting to retrace
what was on the blackboard last night. A list of words
that ought to rhyme (fear and pear, worse and horse,
great and threat) and an outline of a boy eating ice.
Which one's harder, to remember or to forget?
Before the printing press, we had to memorize ideas
or memorialize them in stained glass. Art had a function:
scenes from Beowulf painted. The beatitudes
emblazoned in mosaic. Every object, a plea to memory—
but even with all that effort, it's harder to forget.
It happens only by accident, and the more you want it,
the more you obsess. My ex-wife used to sing a lullaby,
"Never forget me." Tethered to this imperative,
she successfully possessed me. Then divorced and regretted me.
Alzheimer's patients recite poems in an attempt to access
old memories. *Fear works its witchy runnels through a brain
parched hard with thought.* Give it up. Escape. Post-traumatic
stress after a weekend in Las Cruces. I want to forget;
I dream of a clean slate. Unparch me, annul me.
Tabula rasa is my desired state.

POOR SELF OF STEAM

Evaporating in the sauna, in a spa
somewhere in south PA. Spots
of myself become the air. Lifts
from my lungs and hangs in the tropo
sphere. Heir to pools unspooling
on the floor. The tiles divide
and form a prayer. Dear God
it's boring in here. My forehead
is a candle. My hands have been
to war. War of anti-aging bb
creams and vapors that bite like
agent orange. Pour a glacier
through my hair. Dump a Sprite
on these bad pores. Deplore my simile
with agent orange. That'd be fair.
Exfoliants aren't defoliants. Exes
get no remorse. I'm here to fix
myself—to find a way to quit.
But it's hard to quit divorce.

PONDS OF BLONDES

How many syllables are in the words *all alone*. Not one.

How many letters are in the word *letters*?
In all the letters I wrote you last summer?

Three in both o-n-e and h-o-n.

The word *plural* ought to have an *s*
and hello, the word *singular* doesn't need one.

The best food that is also a color is bread. The best food
that is also a verb is flounder, maybe mustered.

We all have that one friend that says
stupid shit like "I like the taste of fruit better than
the taste of candy." I'm sorry

I never wrote you. It's just that I can't
spell *friendship* without also spelling *end*.

The most "blah" color is gravy. The best food that is also a color
that is also a pet name is Honey. My pet's pet name is Antihistamine

but aren't you allergic to dogs? Assign us a sinus infection.
"Eat a colorful plate," my doctor says like a real wise guy.
But glass is just clear. And my doctor's not a guy.

In St. John, we saw a ship full of cargo, also called a shipping ship.
It was in the deep end of the ocean. I'm landlocked

in central Ohio. Hello. This is my S.O.S.

I put the Mel in meltdown. I put the Mel in help me.

A FRENCH INTERIOR

The shrubs rub into leaves, leaves left
in corners, penny red. A dirt path around
the side. A dirty life. Leave it. Think of it,
a cottage: sloping, squat, sodden
battered sky. One lamp limply on, the glow
more gray than gold. Coins pile in corners
carved in shadow; wooden cabinets wink
closed. Old homes have character. Sometimes
they are characters. Holmes is my shelter.
Holden Caulfield is an American Foursquare.
The pages tea-stained, stains steeped
in age. Strewn lily stems as the garden pageant
wanes. Wind me down. I'm winded. Like
the wings of ivy wiping the wisteria green:
Leave me. Close the door on my wooden
unwound quiet. I'm ready for unraveling.
I just don't want to dread it.

MORE MATTER WITH LESS ART

A meadow in lime, mirror-flat.
A meadery in Lima churning vats.
Mirror-cold advances from every
man in Hamlet. More of them
with fewer lines is what the Queen
demanded. It's true that Hamlet
was treated pretty badly, like when
his mom called him a poor wretch
just for walking by and reading.
You've got to be cruel to be kind though,
that's the whole thing. Why not indict
a sitting king? Rosencrantz and Guildenstern
were cast as hyenas in The Lion King.
My dog's name is Ratio, short for
Horatio. I plan my vacations by airport code.
Sleet in Prague and plagued by sleep.
Unplugged lamps loom over unplowed streets.
I make micro-fleece sheets for a living;
my company's name is Microsoft.
New Haven to Helsinki: HVN to HEL.
Fukuoka, Japan to Omaha, Nebraska: FUK OFF.

WHY OUR APARTMENT SHOULD BECOME MY APARTMENT AGAIN

Because it feels like we're buying inventory now for a Best Buy
        that we'll open in the future, and no Best Buy
Will be open in the future, like we're behind the argyle chainlink
That separates this week from next and none of us can climb
Because, and let's be honest, the whole thing is really just
        a horseshoe we found and taped string to
Because we couldn't afford the harp

It's the tragedy of timeshare: the family before us must have taken
        the Scrabble board
Because in each of your eyes there is one shred of pink confetti, and
Confetti has a life of only seconds before it's swept off
Or dead under the couch—because sometimes, coming home
        to you
Is like coming home to an empty house with the fridge door
Left open, and the freezer too, with dinner and dessert
Sliming toward the dog's mouth, only: we don't have a dog
Because you wanted to braid its hair and I wanted a greyhound
So we have candles, and every time I burn one, I open the windows
        and let the trees take the smell on their branches
Like scarves, because we can't keep relying on vanilla bean
        to cover this

This is the decade after the Renaissance and we're a stammering
        fermata
We're the estrangement of a cat's expression when held before a
        mirror
We're spreading earthquake glue on the sidewalk in the middle of a
        hailstorm
We're like 24-hour banking: convenient, but . . .
Thematically, we don't go together
You're the subject-lines of e-mails quarantined in my spam folder

You're the purple wall in the bathroom, and I'm the yellow one
        in the home office, or vice versa, and what's a wall
        to another wall?
Because I feel like we're trying to fly a flag made from saran wrap
Like we're listening to a testimony from the most verbose man
        ever—who has a beard, with food in it
It's a bit like the one illuminating tile in a sod floor, or contacts
        for glass eyes
Like haircuts for fur coats or fur coats just in general

This is pointless, this is a patch of phlox
Yearning along the frame of a black & white movie
This is changing the part in my grandfather's hair and he's
        four-fifths comb-over
Sharing a bathroom with you is like writing an award-winning essay
On what it means to be politically moderate and gay and underwater
Because there's a ring in the toilet and I'm trying to flush it down

Stringent open house, this is the unexplored attic of a cartographer's
        mansion
It's that point in the night when the sky clears its throat, rubs away

The black and waits for the pink sweat of eraser-head
        to bring in the morning
It's that point in the set when the bile-green chanteuse tips off
        the stage corner and toward my
Lonely table: microphone stand slicing her legs while my irrevocable
        fingertips drum, etiolate
I: fragrant bouquet of flagrant carelessnesses, no heels can ride me
Back to where I was with You: pure as unicorns

The first time I lay at the end of the bed and saw how tall you were
Inside, where I crouch and fret, waiting for the latch to fill with key
Warm and scuffed—its nickled head punching through
        your back pocket
Like a peninsula, fighting the urge to drop

THE VOICE OF TRAUMA

is teeth and weed, bleach and scheme. Is timothy welded
to the wrought iron gate. Or Timothy, age eight, still not
weaned. I mean a real boy. They call him Moth,
not Tim, on account of the wings. Call his mother Tulip
Twenty-tulip. You get the gist. She has flowers tattooed
on the insides of her wrists. Petals bloom into letters
bloom into numbers and loom over the heads
of the indebted. The embittered. Which is she. And he?
Not better. A moth is a symbol of allure, truth, and pride.
As in, he truly tried to pry the lid off her worldview.
As in, he bribed a Lowe's worker for some plywood and screws.
Build a cage; open a zoo. He blew through the green
house to get to the cockatoo. Shot through the turnstile
to learn about bamboo shoots. Stole pride from the lions
because he needed to. Meanwhile mom kneeled to pray
at the bathtub tide for some wave to watermark,
waterboard, wave goodbye to their W-2s.

MORE PRAISE FOR STEPHEN KING

Or do I mean Stephen Hawking.
Or do I mean Tony Hawk.
Or do I mean Rick Hawksley, my local councilman,
who called me after I left my ballot blank.
Remember when having a cell phone
meant you had to answer it?
Even if you were sleeping or sledding or
reading Cell? Stephen King hates the movie
adaptation of The Shining. To be fair, Kubrick
did fuck it up. Not enough gleam.
Who is the one who spends all his time
in the deep sea filming squid? Talk about
going to the ends of the earth. Talk about
fishing for meaning. Save yourself some time
searching—Pet Sematary is spelled
with an "S." Apparently, like me, he stole
this: I have the heart of a small boy.
I keep it in a jar on my desk.

RED BADGE OF COURAGE

I read once that courage was red. That in order to breed
birds, you have to also breed bread. That to duck
is a sign of weakness. That living a week during winter
is a sign of depression. That no one knows
the answer to the first yes or no question. That *might*
as used in the Bible does not always mean *maybe,* but *smite*
cleaves consistently. I read that spending the day reading
is lazy, which seems right, that the Patwah word for good sex
is agony. I didn't read but once asked if the halftime show
could be halved and the game eliminated completely.
The cult for the Colts needs to be quartered back. I read that
one pill acts as more of a comfort than a bag of cash.
That water is bulletproof, bullets are waterproof, but it's
impossible to know how many bowls Bob Marley smoked.
My guess? A lot: I read it's always two words. That toward
and towards are basically the same even though they're not.
That a symbol for metaphor is literally any word.
That a metaphor for cymbals sounding is a fraying cord,
cored apple, stray sword. I read that old stars
don't have iron. That old rivers, like most sinners,
eventually straighten out. Bad apples can become
Braeburns, and burn victims can become firefighters,
illustrating a beautiful life cycle. I read that
to write is to doubt, and to write in all caps is to shout.
I don't doubt IRONING SUCKS but should I
never write it down? The back side of a man's shirt
just below the collar is called the yoke, and the space
above the collar is called his head. Both are impossible
to mend. I read that Ford really stands for
Found On Road Dead. I love car jokes. Here's another:
The Chevy Nova didn't sell in Mexico because
in Spanish nova means "doesn't go."
I prefer the cars that compliment: Fit, Ascender,

Liberty, You're the Best. No money down and sign
at the x. Cosine and tangent. Solve for your exes.
They chose to lose you; you choose the lost ones.
I read that you singed a hole in the Friends song.
Sign, sing, singe, sting, stop stringing me along.
I read to bury the hatchet, to burn the urn full of ashes.
Axes and berries and Boston ferns all askew
in your basket. I have something to ask you
and I'm serious so I'll ask it. Everything in print
(your books, manuals, and pamphlets) I want
to revamp them. I want to unread your words,
to unfasten their facets. Get out the matchbook;
bring me the trashcan. Let's make them extinct. Blot out
every letter with a belt of black ink. The blackest.

I AM BOTH WORSE AND BETTER THAN YOU THOUGHT

I put the soul in squalor. I put the lord in dollar.
If I have nothing nice to say, I say it louder.
In all caps on your blog. My dog's name is Paul,
short for APOLOGIZE. I reject Celestial
Seasonings and make my own tea with Stevia
and a bay leaf. A speakable sadness is an
unmoveable feast. The feta doesn't travel well.
My nausea is moon-colored. Stay up late indexing
the little things. ἐχω χάσει τα αυγὰ και τα καλάθια.
The equivalent of "It's all Greek to me" in Greek.
In German, they say, "I can only understand
train station," and then probably, "Ich weiss nicht."
Takes one to know one. Takes gum to blow one.
A bubble. A moon. Floating over the pond
like nausea, the feta swells in the heat.
The back of the Windstar smells like childhood.
I ought to praise you like I should.

DEFINITIONS OF EXCESS

More than the neck of space between screen and glass
where a moth thumps its ragged plea; more than casted shadows
spindled down, unpeeling from the eaves.
Not quite a moat strangling mortar with a muddy stronghold
rink, nor how a stole engulfs a throat, pink throats
of a dozen white minks. If not all this
then touch: the startling flash
from a summer's hose, or the valiant crutch of summer itself
saving us winter's arrows. Now I hear them
before anything else: mouse-eared
chickweed, dribble of gasoline, at Mount Bromo
the regular growl on top the toppling scree.
Without a seat our queen: words like a wedding tent
the night before the ceremony,
till we slink in, buzzing with punch and magnanimity.

MISS NEEDLES & THE DIVORCE

Nerves laced over him like blisters: Mr. Hypochondriac
in the bedroom. Of pools and fact and spume and tact.
He had none of it. Lace nerving against her chest
like glue. In every nativity, he pictured himself
in the manger, too. She saw him standing at the gates
of One Screw Loose. He spat intellect, wading in ego.
He wore suede, sewed business cards, sang manifestoes—
*My wife with a collarbone like a second hand, with a hand
like the Finger Lakes.* In the basement of the flood,
she finally felt safe. Outside clouds hung
like dumb monks. Miles spun from her clumped dot.
She was ineffable, he was uneffable, and so the braid
of their marriage became a black knot. Like a seizure,
an anvil, his temper plaquing sweat. Do you have
to be erect to love like that, or just a wreck?

YOURS

I am your lather, your litter, your hamster, and Brita.
Your first exit, the raw edit, a blank cassette
and basement carpet. Your sinkhole, your cipro,
your perfect Monday cup of joe—aspartame
but hold the cream, a nest of gum and a UFO.

I'm in the details, the slaw, the tide and cesspool.
Beneath your roof's slate, behind this word's fate,
I'm the exception to your number one rule.
Your rubies, your birthstone, the city of your birth,
I am a brothel of lost brothers, a buried urn
full of dead earth. A backyard walnut, your
neighborhood Wal-Mart and the Viet Nam Wall,
all at once. I'm your underwire, you're under fire,
your terrorism and your hunch.

Bonedry, bonewhite, I'm bow resin
and hot air. Your horoscope, your horomones,
I'm Florida this time of year. Your marbles
and marvel, your alarm with fluorescent blaring,
I wrote myself into your book, that nightmare
on marrying: *I do, I do*—your porch columns,
lemonade, your made-for-TV bad eBay trade—
I'm your heteronormative childhood dollhouse,
in a word, I'm harrowing.

Rawhide to bromide and tooth-white fluoride,
I'm your orange rind, bad rhyme, fat black
magpie. Step back in time or reread the lines,
I'll be your very own Gertrude Stein: *I repeat,
there is no repetition*—only me and your DVDs
and several allusions to Tender Buttons.
Both eyelet and button, I'm the first day

with a new razor. I'm crumbs, stone thumbs
and a dream you'll have later. Your west coast
and your next coat, Mt. Holyoke and unsung
holy notes. I'm a glinting gilded birdcage,
but I let the bird go.

I'm your magpie, your meatless pie
and meet me at three: your opponent
in mesh, vanishing in grass: that's me.
Both beagle and bugle, worth millions
as Breughel's Babel—
I'm an ellipse, an eclipse, a list and long
lisp, I'm *it*, don't you see?

Your Mother Confessor, your volume
and possessor, I'm your horse growing hoarse,
your fourth story floorboards, pro-beer
but anti-Coors. O glittering white-throated
shores, ain't gonna do mine but I'll do
your chores—ma petite fleur,
dear reader, sweet juror, I'm yours.

CREDITS

The italicized line in "The Brain Names Itself" is from James Joyce's *Ulysses*.

"Cross Examination" is for Jody Rambo. The poem's first line, set in italics, is borrowed from her poem, "Exit."

"Mother is Only One Letter from" includes lines from Adrienne Rich's poem "Diving into the Wreck" ("Find our way back to this scene, carrying a knife, a camera, a book of myths"), Rich's book *Woman Born: Motherhood as Experience and Institution* ("My children cause me the most exquisite suffering"), and Joyce's *Ulysess* ("yes I said yes I will Yes").

"Gravity & Graves" is written after Chris Kraus's *Gravity & Grace*, a film made after Simone Weil's book of the same title.

"Death Die Dead" mentions Macon Dead, a character from Toni Morrison's *Song of Solomon*.

The title "Pry the Lid off the Terrarium" takes its name from a poem by Matthea Harvey, "The Future of Terror / 3."

"Yes is Not the Only Living Thing" is the inverse statement of an E.E. Cummings line, taken from his poem, "a people shaped toomany-ness far too."

"The French Interior as the Voice of Trauma," "The Voice of Trauma," and "A French Interior," were named after Chris Kraus's ideas on language tense and trauma which are shared in her novel, *Torpor*. "The French Interior as the Voice of Trauma" ends with a quote from Oscar Wilde.

"Oprah's Dowry" begins with a line from Anne Carson's "The Truth about God."

The title "'Maybe, Maybe' (Meaning Maybe Not)" is from Proust's *Swann's Way*.

The title "Miracle Baby Born with a Job" is a headline taken from *The Onion*.

"V.D." is indebted to Beck's *Midnite Vultures* album, particularly the song "Milk & Honey": "I can smell the V.D. in the club tonight."

"If I Were the Moon, I Know Where I Would Fall Down" is a line from D.H. Lawrence's novel *The Rainbow*. "Let me go into the church—alone" is a line from Alfred Hitchcock's *Vertigo*.

The title of "Her Soul Had No Stripes" comes from D.H. Lawrence's novel, *The Rainbow*, as do the lines "a sharp little moon," and "like a drowning, a vagueness."

"Winchester Trilogy" is written for artists Theresa Duncan and Jeremy Blake, RIP. The lines, "It's true that language created even the first ever illumination, and now we borrow back a little word and a little wattage—" come from Theresa's blog. "The sand's ignored BEWARE OF THE UNDERTOW signs" come from the poem "The Sunset" by Randall Mann, also quoted on her blog.

The italicized lines in "Forgetting I'd Already Forgotten" come from Caki Wilkinson's poem, "Suppositions for Skeptics."

"More Matter with Less Art" is a line from *Hamlet*. Many lines in the poem refer to the play.

The line "What's a wall to another wall?" from "Why Our Apartment Should Become My Apartment Again" is indebted to James Tate's poem, "I Take Back All My Kisses."

"I have the heart of a small boy. I keep it in a jar on my desk" from "More Praise for Stephen King" is commonly attributed to King. Robert Bloch, the author of *Psycho*, actually wrote these lines.

The title "I Am Both Worse and Better than You Thought" is taken from Sylvia Plath's journals. The lines, "If I have nothing nice to say, I say it louder. In all caps on your blog," were inspired by the title of a *This American Life* episode, "If You Don't Have Anything Nice to Say, SAY IT IN ALL CAPS." The poem also includes a line from the reality TV program, *Worst Cooks in America* ("feta doesn't travel well"), and ends with a Fatboy Slim lyric.

The first words of "Yours"—"I am your lather"—are borrowed from Kary Wayson's poem "American Husband."

These poems, and so much more, are for Pete.

Thank you to Allison Helmuth, Jody Rambo, Anthony Madrid, Ted Trautman, Kathy Fagan, and Natalie Shapero.

Thank you Kyle and Nick for choosing this one.

Thank you to my mom, Karen Barrett, and my dad, Don Barrett, for the writing desk, the millions of books, and the boundless love that has guided me my entire life. Thank you also to Laura, Donnie, Caroline, and Katie.

Camilla, I love you.

ACKNOWLEDGMENTS

Animal Shelter: "Winchester Trilogy"

apt: "Yours" and "Definitions of Excess"

Better: "The Voice of Trauma," "A French Interior," "The French Interior as the Voice of Trauma"

BOMB: "Noon Says No Twice," "Mother is Only One Letter from," and "Wine Dark and See Thru"

Crazyhorse: "Cross-Examination," "My Life," and "Gravity & Graves"

Gulf Coast: "If I Were the Moon, I Know Where I Would Fall Down"

Harvard Review: "Lived on Decaf, Faced no Devil"

The Iowa Review: "The Brain Names Itself," "I am Both Worse and Better than You Thought," "Asbestos at Best," "More Praise for Stephen King," "Death Die Dead," "Ponds of Blondes," and "Skinny Wisdom"

The Journal: "WFM: Allergic to Pine-Sol, Am I the Only One"

Jerry: "Boy Eating Ice" and "Yes is Not the Only Living Thing"

jubilat: "Warlier" and "More Matter with Less Art"

Narrative: "Paraclete," "Rhymes with Thigh Gap," "Maybe, Maybe (Meaning Maybe Not)," "Poor Self of Steam," "Pry the Lid off the Terrarium," and "Red Badge of Courage"

New Orleans Review: "Her Soul Had No Stripes"

No Tell Motel: "Why Our Apartment Should Become My Apartment Again"

The Paris-American: "Miss Needles & The Divorce"

Pinwheel: "Forgetting I'd Already Forgotten"

Smartish Pace: "Oprah's Dowry"

Sonora Review: "Miracle Baby Born with a Job"

Spooky Boyfriend: "V.D."

"WFM: Allergic to Pine-Sol, Am I the Only One" was reprinted in *Best American Poetry 2015* and *New Poetry from the Midwest 2017*. "Paraclete" was reprinted in *New Poetry from the Midwest 2015*.

The cover art is a painting, *Thimble,* by Pete Burkeet.

Melissa Barrett was born in Cleveland in 1983 and grew up in Kent, Ohio. Her poems and essays have been published in *BOMB, Crazyhorse, Harvard Review, jubilat, Animal Shelter,* and *Best American Poetry 2015*. A Pushcart Prize nominee, her writing has been recognized by the Ohio Arts Council, the Dorothy Sargent Rosenberg poetry prizes, *Tin House*'s Summer Workshop, *Narrative, Gulf Coast,* and *The Iowa Review*. She lives in Columbus, Ohio with her partner, artist Pete Burkeet, and their daughter Camilla.

CPSIA information can be obtained
at www.ICGtesting.com
Printed in the USA
LVHW092315220719
624829LV00002BA/193/P